# FIND YOUR IDEAL EMPLOYEE

How To Consistently Find Great
Staff For Your Business

Brad Flynn

Copyright © 2020 Brad Flynn

All rights reserved

The characters and events portrayed in this book are fictitious. Any similarity to real persons, living or dead, is coincidental and not intended by the author.

No part of this book may be reproduced, or stored in a retrieval system, or transmitted in any form or by any means, electronic, mechanical, photocopying, recording, or otherwise, without express written permission of the publisher.

ISBN-13: 9780648720263

Cover design by: Brad Flynn
Printed in Australia

*To all my clients, I am both privileged and honoured to be part of your incredible journeys. You are the reason I do what I do. I am eternally grateful for your trust and what you have taught me.*

# CONTENTS

Title Page
Copyright
Dedication
About The Author
1. THE GOLDEN RULES OF RECRUITMENT — 3
2. DEFINE YOUR IDEAL EMPLOYEE — 13
3. CONTINUOUS EASY RECRUITMENT — 22
4. INTERVIEWING IN THE NEW MILLINEUM — 34
5. GETTING ROCKSTAR PERFORMANCE FROM YOUR EMPLOYEES. — 46
6. CONCLUSIONS — 51
7. GETTING HELP TO MAKE THIS YOUR REALITY? — 52
Books By This Author — 53

CONTENTS

# ABOUT THE AUTHOR

Businessman, father, husband, keynote speaker, book lover, community builder, pilot… And Author

Brad's journey to date has been nothing like he thought it would be when he left school in a small country town. Gaining a degree in electrical engineering and being involved with projects like Sydney 2000 Olympics before progressing into his own businesses.

Since 2010 he has mentored thousands of business owners with his wealth of street-smart and quickly applicable strategies in helping small business owners build the business of their dreams.

He is the author of **How To Work On Your Business (and not just in it)** that shows business owners exactly what they need to build thier ideal business as well as how to find the time to do it.

He is the author of **Find Your Cash** which includes an online system helping business owners to dramatically boost the cash flow and profitability in their businesses.

He is also the creator of the online **Find My Fee** system, a resource for business coaches and consultants to help clearly demonstrate their value and return on investment to clients in the first meeting.

Since its release in 2019 the system has found on averge more than $100,000 in extra cash for the more than 600 businesses owners around the world in every industry you can think of. For more information visit **www.findmyfee.com**.

**To Apply To Be Mentored By Brad, Scan The Qr Code Below.**

*"Most employees are motivated, energetic, committed, enthusiastic and loyal... Except for the 8 hours they work for you."*

*- Tom Peters*

# 1. THE GOLDEN RULES OF RECRUITMENT

Your Perpetual Recruitment Machine (PRM)

*Because the worst time to recruit is when you have no choice.*

I really didn't need this.

It was just after 5pm on a Friday afternoon. All week, she had been acting very different to normal, I knew something was up and my guts were churning.

There was a light knock on the door of my office.

"Come in" I replied.

"Have you got a minute?" It was Jane and my heart sank.

"Sure come in and pull up a pew. What's on your mind?" I chirped, naively hoping my positivity may overcome the sinking feeling of what I was dreading Jane would say next.

She had been with our business for almost 5 years and was the dream employee, a unicorn in our industry.

Her quality of work was outstanding, only exceeded by her can do attitude.

Please don't tell me you are leaving us, was all I could think.

What was worse was we were heading into our peak season. Trying to find another Jane would be like finding a needle in a haystack at such short notice.

As Jane sat down, she pulled out a tissue and wiped a tear from her eye.

"You know how grateful I am for having been a part of your business, but the time has come for me to move on."


Has this ever happened to you?

I can't tell you the number of times I have heard this story and the massive stress that it inevitably causes for a business owner.

The worst time to recruit or hire new staff is when you absolutely have too.

The stress that this kind of situation causes includes sleepless nights, poor concentration and a snappy boss, as you wrestle with this crisis.

This book was written for you if you are sick and tired of going through this cycle.

The key to breaking this repeating pattern is to follow what I call Golden Rules of Recruitment.

## Golden Rule No. 1 – Always Be Recruiting

The first reaction I get when I tell my clients about Golden Rule No.1 is, "But Brad, what if we don't need anyone."

Lets be clear on what I mean by recruiting.

By recruitment I mean everything in this recruitment process apart from actually hiring someone.

As long as we state that we may not have a position immediately and that we are preparing for when we do then that is quite OK.

If you have a great business that quality people would like to work for, then they will be prepared to wait for that opportunity.

The beauty of this process is if you come across a candidate who doesn't want to wait and is only interested in getting a job now then they have promptly just deselected themselves.

The Perpetual Recruitment Machine (PRM) incorporates many simple life principles that you will learn about as you read on. One of these being...

*The way we do anything is the way we do everything.*

If we have been open and honest with our candidates about how we are working and they have a problem with that, then there is a good chance they will find plenty of other things to have a problem with, if we gave them a job.

Have a think about some of the problem employees you have had or worked with in the past (or even friends or others you know for that matter).

Always be recruiting doesn't mean that you have to be always running paid adverts and interviewing every single person who shows interest.

The PRM is about leveraging technology and other online systems to do the majority of the heavy lifting, so that we will only be speaking to high quality candidates who would be a valuable asset for our business.

Think of it as being like planes being in a holding pattern at the airport.

We will be attracting candidates who, if they make it through the PRM, will be put in a holding pattern for when they are cleared to land in our business. In the meantime they are free to do what they wish.

How would things be in your business if you knew you had holding patterns full of quality candidates for the most important roles in your business, just waiting for you to land them in a role with you when you need them?

This is also particularly powerful if you are looking to rapidly grow and scale your business.

Once you have a business that is running smoothly and profitably (read my book Find Your Cash for how to do that), your most important task then becomes finding great team members and helping them be the best they can be in a role they love and find meaningful, so they can grow your business for you. Its a win win situation.

**Golden Rule No. 2 – Hire Slow, Fire Fast**

Hiring people too fast can be a very expensive mistake, not only financially but also with regard to team culture. Having the wrong person on your team can be a bit like how the bad apple spoils the bunch.

You and the team are not happy because your new team member doesn't fit in and can't do the job they were hired to do, with everyone else having to pick up the slack.

Not only that, there is a very good chance that the new team member is not happy either.

This can be a lose-lose situation.

Stephen Covey, the author of the highly successful book 7 Habits Of Highly Effective People, offers wise counsel to seek and find the win-win or its not deal.

Having an in depth recruitment system to make sure you find the right person for your business is what the PRM is all about.

An integral principle of the PRM can be explained in the Attitude, Knowledge and Skill (AKS) model on the next page.

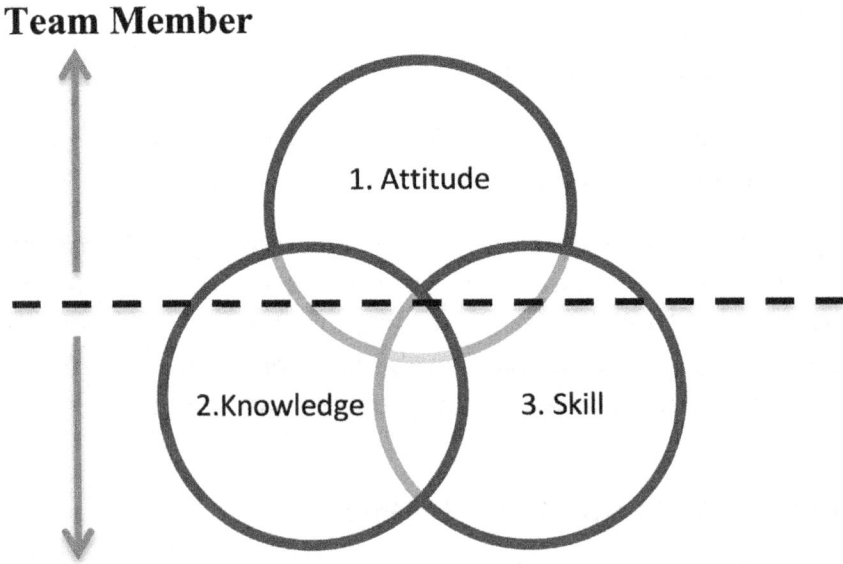

So lets walk through how this model applies to the PRM.

## 1. Attitude

If you were to ask the majority of business owners and employers, what is the most important thing you are looking for when it comes to people who work for you, they will say attitude, thus the heart symbol.

The PRM is about recruiting for attitude primarily, because if someone has the right attitude we can generally train for the skill and knowledge. The caveat on this is there must be at least a solid base of skills and knowledge for the position, particularly certain qualifications if they are required.

You will notice the arrow above the dotted line that is pointing to the team member. That is because the team member is solely and wholly in charge of his or her own attitude. As business owners, we can't control this, only influence it.

As we progress, you will understand the different points at which people will have the opportunity to demonstrate their attitude, through the decisions they make and the actions they take.

It usually becomes apparent quickly those who have an attitude that will not match the culture of our business, so we need to deselect them as an option.

## 2. Knowledge

This is what the person knows, represented by the brain. All learning is directed around helping people to absorb information and then be able to know what to do in applying that information in different parts of their life.

The knowledge can come from a variety of different sources;

1. Formal educational
2. Informal education
3. Previous employment
4. Life experiences (including mistakes)
5. Family and friends

But knowing how to do something is only half of the equation.

You can't learn to swim without getting wet, which leads us to our next point.

## 3. Skills

Skills are the ability to be able to effectively apply knowledge to produce a desired outcome, thus the hand symbol.

The arrow down from the dotted line points to the business owner. It is our job to ensure the candidate has the commensurate level of knowledge and skills to be able to do or at least learn quickly how to do, the job we are hiring for.

It also continues to be on us if the person is struggling in these two areas, so that we offer them any training they need to make sure they are proficient in these two parts of the role.

At the end of the day, a team member is remunerated to produce specific outcomes. There is no point in having someone with an amazing attitude or knowledge or skill set, if they can't get the job done.

Thus we need all three working together.

Golden rule number two is about making sure we get all three of these elements assessed on the journey through our recruitment process.

The PRM is lot like someone auditioning for a play.

You can picture the director and producer and casting people sitting out in the seats, while the aspiring actor is on stage, trying to prove to them with their audition that they are the best person for the role.

So it is with the PRM and this book.

Our mindset and the process is set up to make people jump through some hoops to prove to us that they are the right person for the job and not that we are desperate and will you please come work for us.

## The Purpose of Your Business

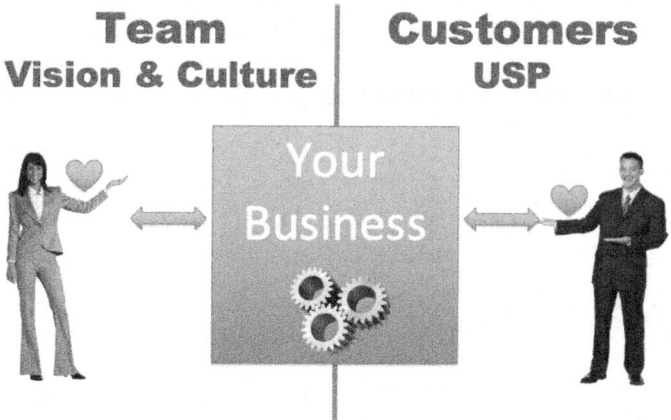

This simple model provides the basis for what an ideal business can look like.

On the left hand side we have our team, who are engaged, enrolled and inspired by the vision we have for our business and our long-term goal. They are committed to and believe in what our business is all about and take great meaning from and pride in their role.

On the right-hand side are our customers and clients, who we provide with exactly what they want also in a meaningful way that is most important to them and is a part of our Unique Selling Proposition (USP). If you breakdown the word unique, it becomes uni- which means one and -que, as in a queue or line or sequence of people waiting to be served.

In other words, we are first in the queue when our clients think of the product or service that we provide.

This synergistic relationship between our team members and our clients is facilitated by our business sitting in the middle.

Our business allows our team to give their unique skills, talents and abilities in a meaningful way, all the while giving our clients exactly what they want by delivering our Unique Selling Proposition (USP).

All the while, your business is the vehicle that provides you with the lifestyle you desire, which is why we went into business for in the first place. I call this triple win. What else could you ask for.

So lets dive into how we find the people to help us make this a reality.

# 2. DEFINE YOUR IDEAL EMPLOYEE

"Gentlemen, we can rebuild him, we have the technology and capability to build the world's first bionic man" – Oscar Goldman

## The 6 Million Dollar Man

My favourite show growing up was the 6 Million-Dollar Man. It was about the bionic man Steve Austin.

The US government had a top-secret operation that was around creating the ultimate agent.

Austin who nearly dies in a serious accident, is saved and rebuilt with a bionic right arm, a bionic leg and bionic eye, all of which gave him superhuman strengths and power.

They had built the perfect secret agent.

He was already an intelligent person and now with super strength he was able to do amazing things and always solve the crime. (The bionic woman show was just as cool by the way.)

This is exactly what we want to do as we build roles for the various positions in our business.

If you could build the equivalent of your own 6 million dollar team member, what are the various traits and strengths you would like them to have?

You may be able to find everything you want in one person, but more often than not, you may need to take various parts that you are seeking, from various people.

Kind of like a recipe for your favourite dish.

We call this ideal reference for the position, an avatar.

So, grab a pen and paper and start a brain dump as we begin building your 6-million-dollar employee.

Don't worry too much about formatting at this stage, just get as much down on paper as you can as your starting point.

Here are some different areas for you to consider as you build your avatar.

1. Existing team members

    - Who are your existing team members who may be a good model to build your avatar around? What are some of their individual strengths (think bionic arm)?

    - What are some of the negative traits of current or past team members that you want your avatar to have the opposite of?

2. Other employees in other businesses.

    - Are there other employees you know in other businesses who have traits you like?

    - What about people you have worked with in the past and admired how they did their work.

3. Yours or other company's values and culture

    - What are some of the words and traits you are looking for. E.g.

        - Honesty
        - Integrity
        - Takes ownership
        - Problem solver
        - Creative
        - Team player
        - Loyalty
        - Empathy
        - Punctual
        - Attention to detail
        - Outgoing
        - People person

So how is your list going?

In the later chapters we will begin covering how you can filter for these various traits by asking the right questions.

## Behavioral Profiling

Hands down, one of the most important tools in your PRM tool kit is the use of behavioral profile tools.

There are many different types of these assessment tools that can give you important information into how a person is likely to behave in certain circumstances. This can potentially save you thousands of dollars in a bad hire for a relatively minor investment for the assessment, which can be done online before you even meet a candidate.

My preferred behavioral profile assessment is called DiSC and in the next couple of sections I will give you a basic overview and how it applies to selecting your ideal team member.

## What Disc Do You Need?

There are 4 main traits for the DiSC profile. Whilst we all have varying degrees of each of the 4 traits, we can quickly assess someone or what kind of person will be best for our role by asking 2 simple questions.

Is the person outgoing or reserved?
Is the person task or people focused?

This will then land the person in one of 4 quadrants that will have certain traits. See the following matrix.

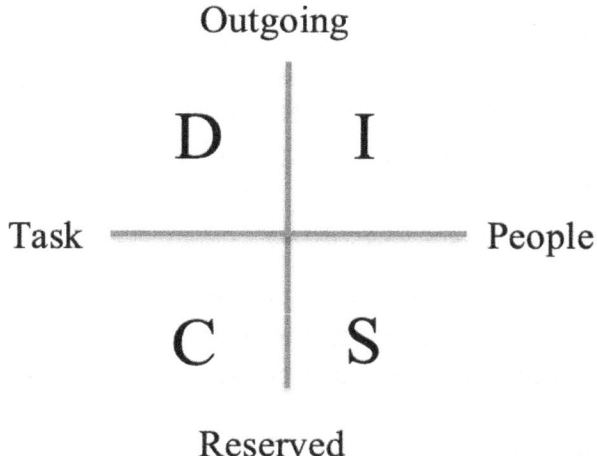

## D – Dominance

- Outgoing and task focused
- The D behavioral style is dominant and direct
- They like change and being in charge
- Results oriented, like to win
- Dislikes being taken advantage of

This particular style is best suited for roles where there is a bit of competition and very heavily results and outcome oriented. Think CEO's, executive, and operational managers.

## I – Influence

- Outgoing and people focused
- The I behavioral style is about influence
- They are enthusiastic and love people
- Pride themselves on influencing others
- Dislikes being rejected

This style is all about getting their results by influencing others. They are inspiring and charming and love being around people. Think sales, customer service, retail, receptionist and public relations.

## S – Steadiness
- Reserved and people focused
- The S style is about steadiness and stability
- Even tempered and agreeable
- Doesn't like change
- Dislikes loss of security

The S style can be a bit like the shock absorbers in organisations. They remain calm and steady in most situations and will steadily complete their role. Think nurses, counselors, assistants and HR.

## C – Conscientiousness
- Reserved and task focused
- The C style is analytical and detail oriented
- Likes lots of data and information
- Is very systematic and precise
- Dislikes criticism

The C style is all about using information to make decisions. They think logically in the way they make decisions and can be very objective. Think accountants, engineers, software and analysts.

If the traits and values we reviewed in the first part of this chapter are all about <u>why</u> people tend to do what they do, the behavior profiling is all about the <u>how</u> they do things.

The temptation for most business owners is to go looking for the ultimate person who has all traits and can do all things.

Generally, the reference they are using is themselves, because as a business owner you have to be able to do everything when you first begin your business.

The big danger with this is that if you do find someone who can do everything, the chances of them learning as much as they can from you and then going and starting their own business can be quite high.

The caveat to this is that if the person did have their own business and decided it wasn't what they wanted to do with their life. These people can make ideal employees because they fully understand the challenges of the business owner and thus can be loyal and make a great contribution.

**The Position Description (Pd)**

Up until now we have been developing the attitude element of our AKS (Attitude, Knowledge and Skills) model, the heart of our avatar.

Now it is time to switch our focus to the actual position that we are looking to fill, in other words the knowledge and the skills that our avatar must have, the brains and the hands to do the work.

PD's are largely composed of three major areas.

1. The key responsibilities and accountabilities and how they are measured.

2. The skills and attributes the person must have, including qualifications and knowledge.

3. The relationships internally and externally that the person will have in the role.

The other critical thing that a PD must have that is often overlooked is a measure of the performance that the position and thus the business needs.

The first thing we must be very clear on is...

**What Exactly Are We Paying Someone For?**

Like the win-win or no deal principle we discussed earlier, we need to work out what a win-win will look like in this instance.

What will the win for the business look like and what will the win for the team members look. The PD will set the standards to make this happen.

The first and most important question we need to ask is "what is the number 1 thing we are paying the person to do, for who the PD relates to?"

This is where most PD's fail.

We must be able to measure what we decide the number 1 thing is. This measure is sometimes called a Key Performance Indicator (KPI).

At the highest level, all businesses provide one of the following.

1. Products – something physical
2. Services – usually time based
3. A combination of the above two.

Which one is your business providing to your market?

Once you know what you provide to your market, we can go deeper on working out what the key elements are that contribute to the delivery of your solution to the market.

The second biggest mistake I see in PD's is too much information.

If a PD only needs one KPI, then so be it. It doesn't need to have a bunch of fluffy irrelevant information just to make it a certain number of pages. If you pay someone to do one thing in this position, then that is all you need.

Here is a few of the more common KPI's that can be used to measure performance;

- Units produced
- Hours invoiced
- Sales generated
- Units delivered
- Quote estimate vs actual cost
- Profit per job
- Referrals

Once you have worked out the number one thing you pay the person to do in this role, then move on to second most important thing, then the third and so on.

We are now able to define the first and most important part of the PD, what the key responsibilities are and how they are measured. After all, this is what we pay this person to do.

The next section of the PD is where we list out the Skills and the Knowledge that are required to be able to adequately (and sometimes legally) complete the role.

And the final section of the PD is about the relationships that the person will have within the business and externally.
For instance, if they interact with the administration team, this would be an internal relationship whereas dealing with suppliers is an example of an external relationship.

With our avatar now clearly defined in terms of their attitude (heart), skills (hands), knowledge (brains), DiSC behavioral style and position description, we are now able to start attracting the right people to our organisation who fit the bill and help us build our dream team.

# 3. CONTINUOUS EASY RECRUITMENT

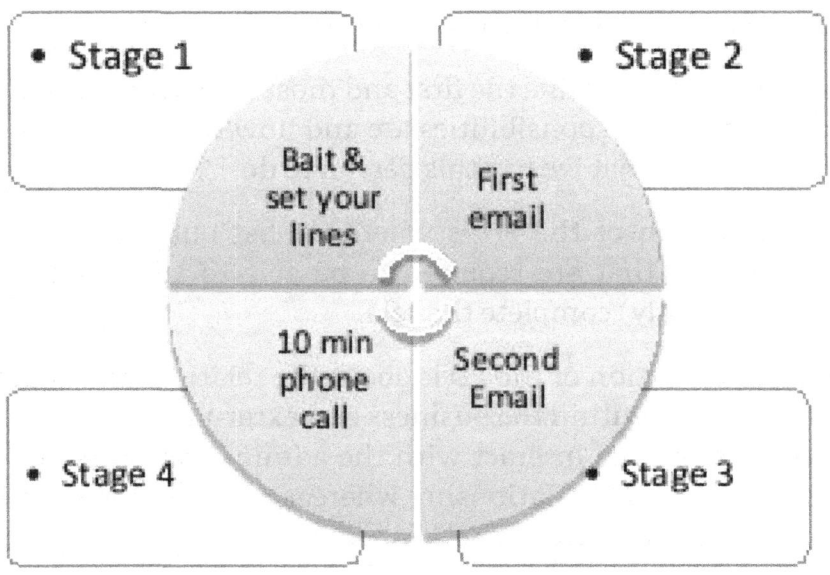

"People run the systems,
Systems run the business,
You lead your people."
- Michael E. Gerber

We used to go camping out in the bush, to a place called the Rocky River.

It was real camping. No power. Sit around the fire and cook your food on it, take the shovel and go for a walk if nature called.

All the while we would set up our fishing lines along the river.

Then every hour or so we would go back and check them, to see if we had a fish or we needed to re-bait the hooks and try again.

This is a lot like what we need to be doing with this stage of the PRM. In fact fishing is a great analogy for finding our ideal candidates. You need to know what bait to use, where to place your fishing line, what tide is best, what time of the year and so forth.

Now we are clear on what type of candidates we want to attract from our last chapter, let's start setting up some ways for them to make contact with us.

**Stage 1 – Bait And Set Your Lines**

**The Bait**

When a fish goes past the bait, if it is hungry and likes the look of the morsel on the hook, you have got its attention.

And so it is with getting the attention of our avatar.

Think about how you decide what it is that you are going to read either in a newspaper or online.

The first thing that grabs our attention is the headline or a picture. This is usually because the words or image, match something important to us in our consciousness. So we hone in on it and then take the next step.

The next step is to read the subheading or the first paragraph of the article or post. If this further engages us based on what our interests or values are, we read on.

Then the article goes into more detail giving us some more information about the topic.

The difference between a newspaper article and a job advert is we have a call to action at the end of the advert.

This is exactly how we want to write our advert for attracting the attention of our avatar.

For example, if we were looking for an administration assistant, we could come up with an advert something like this...

## Wanted: Motivated Administration Assistants with an attention to detail.

If you are the administration assistant we are looking for, and likes being part of a friendly team who believe in our products and services, this position maybe for you.

At Sample Company, we are dedicated to working with our clients and providing the best samples in the market place, whilst having an amazing place for us to work and grow.

Some of the tasks you will be carrying out include;

- Answering the phone and booking appointments for our clients
- Supporting the management team
- Receiving deliveries
- Greeting clients on arrival

If this sounds like you, then send us an email to jobs@sampleco.com and we will be in touch. (Please no resumes at this stage)

So as you can we had a headline that was targeted to who we want the attention of.

We then gave some more information about why Sample Company is a great employer as well as some of the tasks the person would be performing.

And finally we gave them a call to action, for how they can apply for the job.

Note that I said not to include resumes at this stage, a simple test to see if they can follow instructions. There will be more on this to come.

**Now set the lines.**

Continuing with the fishing metaphor, now we need to set our lines. In other words place our advert in various locations where our ideal avatars may be hanging out and who may want to become part of our great team

When you are fishing, you will feel a little tug on the line, a nibble.

In our situation, if someone is interested in finding out more about the opportunity to work with us, is when they send us an email to the specific hiring email address in the advert.

Here is a list of a few different locations you can set your lines.

1. Your website

By having a specific page set up on your website with your job advert from above, you can tell potential candidates a little bit more about why being part of your team is such an amazing opportunity and obviously a bit more about the position.

However, we don't want to go into too much detail here. The object here is attracting as many candidates as we can and let the system do the heavy lifting.

2. Vehicle signage

Depending on the nature of your business, if you have vehicles that are out and about on the road, having a simple decal is all you need.

Something like;

*We are hiring, email us at jobs@sampleco.com*

### 3. Newsletters

Make sure at the bottom of your newsletters, you have a snippet around looking for great people to work for you. Having team member profiles in newsletters is always a winner as people get to know more about your team, so include the snippet on hiring here.

### 4. Social Media

By having a post every couple of weeks or so, you are able to remind your followers that you are always looking for great people. They may then be able to tag people they know into the post to make them aware.

### 5. Email signatures

As for the newsletters option above, have a subtle hyper link at the bottom of your email letting people know about the opportunity to potentially work for you business. Just like tagging people in social media, the person receiving the email may forward it on to a relevant person.

### 6. Paid Websites

These include sites such as seek.com where you are able to get your job out to a large number of candidates but these sites can be expensive.

These are just a few simple strategies to get you thinking about where you can post.

Where else can you be baiting and setting your lines?

## Stage 2 – Email In

Just because you get a nibble on your bait, doesn't mean you should reef the rod back and starts reeling in like a crazy person. You need to be patient until you are sure you have hooked the fish and bring them in.

Our first nibble is when we get an email in to the specific email address that we have been putting out through our lines.

The reason that we choose a separate specific email for this process is that we want to automate its response. A basic response like below is all that the email we automatically send back needs to say.

*Hi there,*

*Thanks for taking the time to reach out and find out more about working for [insert company name].*

*As you will see we do things a little bit differently, so we need to you make sure you follow our instructions if you are serious about a position with us. At this point PLEASE DON'T SEND US RESUME OR A COVER LETTER.*

*For now, all you need to do is respond to this email with your answer to these 3 questions;*

*1. What do you see as your 3 strongest attributes?*
*2. What is your biggest success? And*
*3. Why do you see yourself as being suited to this position?*

*Please include your best contact number and time during business hours that is best to contact you.*

*We will be in touch soon to let you know what will happen next.*

*Thanks again, we will be in touch soon.*

An alternative to having the candidates send you an email as in the job advert, is to have them call a voicemail service with the above email script as the recording and let them answer the questions by leaving a voicemail.

With this option, you can buy a sim card that fits your existing mobile phone, take your normal sim card and put the new one in then record the above message on it.

Then all you need to do is every few days, put the above sim card back in your phone and listen to the messages and take notes.

Instead of having an email address in the job advert, now you list the mobile number for the sim card.

The answers to the above questions give us our first insight into the candidate.

The answer to Question One gives us an idea of what they see as their personal strengths. This could be skills, knowledge or attitude related.

The answer they provide to the second question provides us with an insight into what is most valuable to this person.

This is of particular importance when it comes to matching someone's values with our company values, also known as company culture.

You will know yourself that if you are ever forced to go against your values it is not a pleasant situation to experience.

Similarly, if we have a new employee who doesn't share a similar values base that our company and existing employees do, we could have a real problem.

Finally, the answer they provide to the last question gives us an idea of what they see within themselves that will be a good fit with our business. It will also provide us with some information to form questions around later.

This now gives us a basis to start to compare the candidate's answers against our avatar. Also, because they have taken the time to respond, it means they have read our email and followed the instructions.

My suggestion however with the timing of responses is, if they take longer than a day or two in responding, there is a good chance they are slow responding to other things (remember my earlier comment about the way we do things?).

Also, if they fail to answer the questions as asked or still send their resume in, even though we asked them not to, they probably will do the same thing if we employ them and not follow our instructions.

If you think the candidate is not a match for the business or the position, kindly let them know in a reply email. All you need to reply with is something simple like;

*Hi [Firstname],*

*Thank you for taking the time to reply to our email and answering our questions. Unfortunately at this stage we will not be progressing. We have your details on file and wish you all the best.*

Now at least the person is not left hanging wondering what happened after their efforts. In the long run if the person was not a fit, we are better moving past it quickly so as not to waste theirs or our time any further.

### Stage 3 – 10 Minute Phone Call.

If a candidate has followed all the instructions and we think they are worth engaging with, now its time for a quick call. They have followed the instructions and given us a number to call them on and a time.

Often having a quick conversation with someone gives you massive insights into the person.

If we are not looking to employ someone straight away, now is the time to let them know too.

This call does not have to be done by the business owner either. It can be carried out by whoever the candidate would be reporting to or someone else from the team, saving the business owner time and energy.

A simple call script and some basic questions can look something like this.

*Hi [Firstname], its [your name] here calling from [company name]. Have you got a moment for a quick chat?*

*Great, thanks for your interest in joining us and your emails.*

*The reason for the call today was to ask you a few more questions to check your suitability for our business and the position and to see if you have any questions. Is that OK?*

*Great. Just so you know, we are currently compiling a list of suitable candidates for when the next position opens up. At this stage we are unsure when that will be, but think it will be within the next [insert timeframe if you have one], is that OK?*

*So tell me a little bit about what you are doing now?*

*How long have you been in your current position?*

*Why did you reach out to apply for a position with us at this point?*

*Tell me a little about your qualifications?*

*And what are your salary/wage expectations.*

*And did you have any questions for us at this point?*

*Thank you for your time today [firstname] we really appreciate the chance to have a quick chat.*

*We will get back in touch with you in the next couple of days to let you know if you have progressed to the next stage or not.*

*In the meantime, have a great day.*

This call shouldn't be a big long chat, although they sometimes can be, which is OK. The point is again to compare the persons answers and the way they conducted themselves on the phone call with our avatar.

If you don't think this person is a good fit for the company or the role, then send them the quick email from the previous stage, within the next day or two as promised.

If you believe they are worth progressing to the next stage, read on.

**Stage 4 – Skills Test.**

Now that we have a large part of the avatars attitude assessed and they have made it to this stage, its time to take a look at some of their skills and knowledge and how they apply them.

The skills test is not about a rigorous examination of every thing that they need to know how to do for the job.

Its about looking at how they think, assess and take action in certain situations.

It can be a written assessment where they have to come in and answer some questions. I don't suggest sending them an online type of assessment for this as they can find the answers if they don't know them on Google.

We also want to put a little bit of pressure on them by having them come in to our office to see how they respond, remember, the way we do anything... It also lets you see the quality of their handwriting and basic grammar, if this is relevant for the position.

Most positions have some kind of task that requires the culmination of a bunch of skills and knowledge to be applied.

For instance.

**Tradies** – is there a certain type of joint, termination, connection or another task that is uncommon and would uncover a person's ability to complete.

**Admin** – maybe you could use a slightly complex task in Word or Excel to produce a certain outcome, like a mail merge or calculation table.

**Professional Service** – think of a tricky situation that has come up for you or a team member in the past to find out how the candidate would handle it.

**Health professional** – similar to the professional service above, think of a complex injury or illness and see how the person would diagnose and treat it. You can also have them do hands on assessment of yourself or another team member as part of the skills test.

**Sales** – set up a sales situation and role play to see how they handle it and what they are like with objections.

**Marketing** – give them a basic brief for a client and see what their thought process is like in coming up with a campaign.

If you feel confident enough at the end of the skills assessment that they are continuing to tick all the boxes, then go ahead and book a time for an interview. Ask them to come dressed as they would for the position and bring a copy of their resume with them.

Otherwise if you need to discuss the candidate with your team or other advisors, commit to getting back to them in a day or so to let them know.

If they are to progress to the interview stage, now is the appropriate time to carry out a DISC assessment and see if there is a match with our avatar.

The final phase of the PRM is the interview, lets take a look at this critical final stage and why it can be so revealing if someone has got this far and are the wrong person.

# 4. INTERVIEWING IN THE NEW MILLINEUM

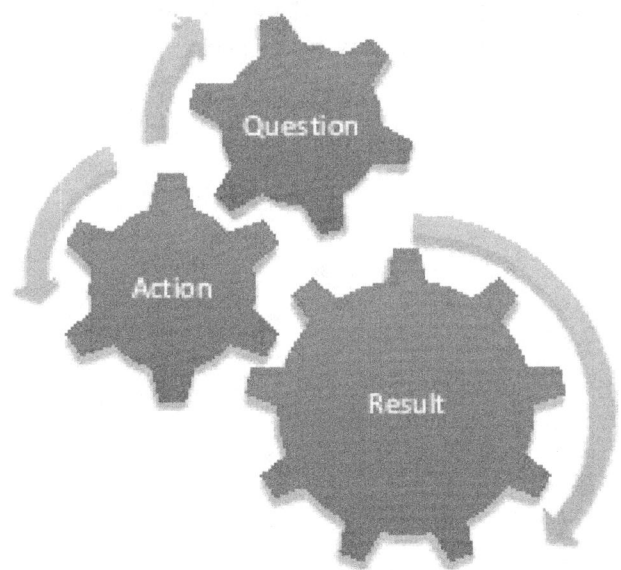

"The quality of your life,
Is determined by the quality of your questions"

*- John Demartini*

There are two key things I believe I am responsible as a parent in preparing my kids for adulthood.

The first thing is a concept called Above and Below the Line, which was originated by a guy called Marshall Thurbur. You can watch my video on YouTube that describes it by searching for 'Brad Flynn above the line.'

This concept is essentially about the decisions we make in our lives and the subsequent actions. We can either take ownership, accountability and responsibility to become the victors of our lives. Or, we can blame, make excuses, be in denial and become the victims of our lives.

No prize for guessing which side of the line is my suggestion to live on.

The second key thing I want my kids to be excellent at, is asking great questions. Not only questions of others but also of asking themselves to reveal deeper insights and learning's about who they are and how to live fulfilling lives.

There are a couple of things that accompany asking great questions though.

First of all is the quality of the knowledge and education, you have achieved to date in your life.

This dictates a lot of what you believe is possible.

And by education I don't mean formal education. Just ask Sir Richard Branson how many degrees he has from university (none).

The quality of your knowledge and education is heavily influenced by whom you have been getting this information from, either purposefully or just by hanging around someone.

You see, you don't need to be in someone's presence to learn from them. We can get it by reading their books, watching their videos or listening to their podcasts or audiobooks.

Ultimately, your education and thus beliefs and knowledge will lead to the quality of the questions you ask and thus the quality of the answers you get.

Think about Google. The better the information or question you give Google to work with, the better the answers it provides.

So lets look at the art of asking great questions and how to apply this important skill in your interviews.

**How To Ask Great Questions**

All questions can be classed into 2 types.

**Type 1 – Closed**

A closed question is quite simply one that can only be answered with a yes or a no. These questions are generally very limiting when it comes to finding solutions or exploring options.

**Type 2 – Open**

An open question is any question that can't be answered with a yes or no. This is the most powerful type of question that we will deep dive on when it comes to our interviews of candidates as they will reveal the most about that person and suitability.

Rudyard Kipling sums it up best with this quote;

> *"I keep six honest serving men*
> *They taught me all I knew*
> *Their names are what and why and when*
> *And how and where and who"*

When I first began learning about the importance of being able to ask great questions, I memorized this saying to help me remember open questions.

All open questions start with one of Rudyard's six honest serving men. Lets break each one down.

**What** – Starting a question with what, is a way of asking for specific information. For instance, "what do you like to do in your spare time?" It is generally looking for a particular outcome to be ascertained.

**Why** – The purpose of a why question is to uncover reasons that led to a specific outcome. When it comes to an individual, this can tell us a lot about their values and the reasons they take certain actions. Because of this, it is often best to use this question when there is a fairly high level of rapport and trust. For example "why do you want to work with us?"

**When** – This type of question relates specifically to time. It can be in the past, present or future context when used in conjunction with other questions too. For example "when can we meet up?"

**How** – How based questions deal with the mechanics of the outcomes of something. For example, "how would you solve problem XYZ?

**Where** – A where based question deals with the location or position of the item being discussed. For example, "where do you see yourself in 5 years?"

**Who** – And finally, the who relates to an individual. For example "who do you admire?"

With this foundation in mind, its...

### Time To Interview

Depending on timing and the level of satisfaction you have with the candidate to this point, it is possible to carry out the interview with skills test.

Even better, a strategy I regularly use with clients is to hold group interviews that includes a skills test element.

This is a very time efficient strategy and the group environment adds that little bit more pressure to the candidates to see how they handle it.

This very much depends on the position you are looking to fill though.

Now let's step through my 5 interview checkpoints to make sure we get the right person for our business.

**Interview Check Point 1 – Punctuality**

Unless there is some major reason that is a long way beyond our candidate's control, they should ensure they are at the interview location ahead of time.

If they are late, even with a very good reason, they have lost me.

In fact, in a group interview situation, if they are late, I lock the doors so they can't get in.

Think about it, if you are serious about the job you really want to get, you make sure you build in adequate time to account for traffic issues and anything else.

I have held interviews where I see candidates turning up 30 minutes before start time.

I have even been known to have team members go and take a look through the windows of their car and see what it like inside.

They lose points if their car is full of fast food wrappings and rubbish. The way we do anything...

**Interview Check Point 2 – Appearance**

This is another example of checking if they listened to the instruction. This element gives us a solid impression for how they will be representing us to our customers if this is part of their role.

Simple things like clothes ironed, hair tidy, and shoes clean and so on, tell us plenty about our candidate.

**Interview Checkpoint 3 – The Overview**

Now it is back over to us.

Once we have greeted our candidate/s, we want to give the candidate a quick overview of how the interview will go. It also gives us a good opportunity to get focused and clear on the direction <u>WE</u> want to take the interview.

A simple script like below is what I usually have my clients use.

*Thanks for coming in today [firstname] to have a chat with us.*

*I just want to give you a quick overview of what we are going to go through for the next 30 minutes or so, is that OK?*

*Great. First of all we will give you a little bit of history about our business and what working here is like.*

*Then we will give you a quick overview of the position and what it entails and some of our expectations.*

*We are then going to ask you a few questions to learn more about you and your suitability for the business and the role.*

*And finally if you have any questions you can ask them after all of that. Does that sound OK?*

You will notice that I checked in with them a couple of times to see if it was OK. Part of this is to help them feel a little bit more at ease and part of it is to see their reaction.

The next script is crucial in the process as we set the tone right from the start. Here is what I will say.

*Now we understand that you may be a little nervous with the interview and that's OK, just do your best.*

*But we ask you to be open and honest with your answers. We have a very well defined process that will pick up if you are not being yourself.*

*You see if you were to fudge your answers and we ended up employing you, there is a good chance you would end up being unhappy as would we, nobody wins and we don't want that do we?*

*So my suggestion is to just be yourself and answer the questions as best you can, does that make sense?*

*Great lets get started.*

**Interview Checkpoint 4 – The Questions.**

When it comes to the questions we ask in the interview, there is one simple principle that will guide us. And that is;

***Past behavior is the best predictor of future behavior***

So our questions need to be directed at asking our candidates to tell us about a time in the past that relates to what we are trying to understand.

The challenge with asking future based questions is that they can easily make up answers and there are no consequences.

Even if they are making up answers about the past, there is a good chance you will sense it or see it in their body language.

One of the most underrated abilities humans don't use enough of, is our intuition. The word literally means, tuition or learning from within.

From an evolutionary perspective, we are wired to pick up anomalies in the communication we receive from those around us.

In prehistoric days, if someone or a group of people approached us who were not from our clan, we needed to be able to work out if they were friend or foe and thus be prepared.

If they were friend then we could work together, one of the things that humans do pretty well most of the time.

If they were a foe, we needed to detect this and be on high alert for any attack.

Thus, over the millennia of evolution this 6$^{th}$ sense has been developed and refined.

I call it my spider senses, when you just get a funny feeling about someone, a bit like spiders can pick things up at a distance, without seeing or hearing what is causing it.

Apologies, I digress, lets get back to the questions.

With all the prep work we have done up to this point, we really only need to ask a handful of questions, usually no more than six at the most. But we want them to really hone in and hit the mark with their answers.

Below are my top 6 questions that tell me most of what I need to know at this point about our candidate, in conjunction with all our other steps and comparing this to our avatar.

### 1. Give me some examples of how your last boss got the best out of you?

This gives you a big insight into how you can get the best out of them should they come on board and if it is something you or your team are capable of doing.

### 2. What was the biggest mistake or most embarrasing moment in your last job? What did you learn?

This is by far the most important question in the whole PRM, for a number of reasons.

For a long time I tried to find a way to work out someone's tendency to play above the line as we discussed earlier.

We all fall below the line at times in life, its part of being human. The name of the game is to be able to catch ourselves and get back up above the line, as fast as we can.

This means being comfortable with being vulnerable and taking ownership, accountability and responsibility.

By asking this question, we give our candidates an opportunity to do just that.

If they fail to take this opportunity then there is a very high possibility they will do the same when working for us.
A person who plays below the line can be destructive to a positive team culture and an absolute nightmare to try and manage.
What would your answer be in that situation?
If you are like most business owners, I have known who play above the line, you will probably chuckle and say, "just one mistake, I have made thousands!"

### 3. What frustrated you most about your last position or job?

If it frustrated them at their last job and it is part of the current role or environment, then it will frustrate them at our business.

### 4. Tell me about a time when you had a difficult customer - how did you handle it and what did you learn?

This will give us an insight into how they handle tricky situations when they are under pressure.

### 5. How do you define a great work atmosphere?

Whilst this question does go against what I said about asking past based questions, it does give us a great reference to see how they will fit in with your work atmosphere and your team.

## 6. What do you think your referees will say?

This again gives you some insight into what their referees are likely to say as well as giving them another opportunity to be a little vulnerable, open and honest.

### What to watch out for with their answers.

Firstly, are they actually answering the questions they were asked directly or are they just waffling on and not giving you a specific answer?
If they are waffling, they have either not been listening to the question or are not able to answer it. In which case they should just be open and honest and say they don't have an answer i.e. be vulnerable.

Secondly, the interviewers must resist the temptation to jump in and try and help the person answer the questions.

This is particularly relevant for the I and S type personality, who don't particularly like uncomfortable silences.

Trying to help them and put words into their mouth is just shooting yourself in the foot (maybe consider where else in your business you are doing this, if this relates to you).

We want to understand how they cope with the pressure on them, because…you know.

### Interview Checkpoint 5 – The Close

Now we are about to start wrapping up. Hopefully you have been able to glean information for comparison to our avatar and assess a fit with the business and team.

Offer them the opportunity to ask any questions they may have. This is also a good opportunity to see how keen they are and how much thought they have put into working here. Big ticks for relevant questions from them.

At the conclusion of the interview we want to thank them and congratulate them for getting this far. If you have some information around how many emails and applicants you had at the front end, let them know.

Finish the interview on a high and have them leave feeling confident about their achievement in getting this far.

Let them know that you will get back to them within the next day or two, as we have done at each stage along the way.

Now spend some time reviewing the notes you have taken, skills tests, DISC assessments and all the other factors and comparing to your avatar.

If there were others in the interview with you, which I always recommend, compare notes.

I always suggest sleeping on it and see how you think the fit is in the morning.

### Resumes & Reference Checks

By this stage you probably have a pretty good idea of if the person is a fit, but I would still proceed with this last important element.

When checking the resume, look for short employment periods and lots of jobs. The obvious question is around why were they jumping around so much.

Also, take a look at the companies they have worked for. You may know someone there who is not listed as a referee who can give you some valuable insights.

Obviously, there are the referees they have listed, but you would fully expect them to say good things otherwise they wouldn't be listed.

Here are some questions to consider asking the referees.

1. How long did [name] work for you?
2. What were their roles?
3. How would you describe their punctuality? What about their reliability?
4. Would you hire them again? Why?
5. What were some of their strengths?
6. What were some of the things they could improve upon?

Most importantly at the conclusion of the call, thank them for their time and input.

Whilst technically not a reference check, it is also a good idea to check social media platforms and do a Google search. This can often reveal interesting elements of someone's character that may be handy to know.

# 5. GETTING ROCKSTAR PERFORMANCE FROM YOUR EMPLOYEES.

*A business never outperforms its leader.*

**"Daddy, Daddy, Close Your Eyes"**

Is this something your kids or children you know have ever wanted to do with you, whilst they take you by the hand and lead you to see something, they want you to see?

Whenever my kids would play this game with me, I would obediently cover my eyes, leaving a little crack between my fingers so I can see where I am going and don't walk into a door, wall or something else.

Kids don't have the spatial awareness that adults do and so are not thinking about what is in your path, consequently if you don't look where you are going you could come crashing down on your adventure.

Whereas if the child had said to you something like...

Ok, there is something I want to show you, but I want it to be a surprise.

I am going to ask you to close your eyes, but first, I am going to tell you about how this surprise will unfold.

We are going to take 5 steps forward, turn left into the hallway, then another 7 steps forward and turn right into my bedroom, then you can uncover your eyes for the big surprise!

Obviously, the chances of the young child doing this are pretty slim, however you would feel a little bit more comfortable closing your eyes fully with no peaking.

It's a bit like this when a new candidate or team member starts either engaging or working with you.

You know exactly where you want them to go, but they have no clue.

You will notice through the book I have regularly given overviews to our candidates about the pathway we would be taking.

This helps them feel a little bit more at ease as well as helping you assess how they are progressing.

So, when somebody starts with us, it is important that we are able to provide them with an overview of where we are going and how we are going to get there.

In fact, leadership in general is about communicating to the team where we are leading them, so they are clear on the journey and can think ahead.

With that in mind lets discuss what happens after the interview on the basis that our candidate has ticked all the boxes and we would like to offer them an opportunity to come and work with us.

**The Job Offer And Induction**

The final phase of the PRM is to offer the candidate the position and then provide them with a solid induction, giving them a strong platform to perform and become part of your team.

The offer is something between you and your new employee, but the key foundation is that it must be a win for you and a win for them.

The thing about the PRM is that you have actually been inducting and positioning the successful candidate, through the whole process.

You have been setting the standards of what is expected even before they signed up. This is one of the powerful parts of PRM process.

Some of the other important things to consider with your induction process include;

> 1. Company policies and procedures document – go through the salient points and have them read and

sign off on this. In particular consider things like annual leave, social media, and smart phone policies and warning and termination procedures.

2. Position Description – make sure they are clear on what their deliverables are and what they will be kept accountable to and they sign off on it.

3. Introductions to direct reports and who they report to.

4. Relevant health, safety and emergency procedures.

5. Relevant training on equipment and software

6. Knowing where they need to go to get help should they need assistance.

Think of the induction procedure as a bit like a pre-nuptial agreement. We want to have all the tough conversations up front, so they are very clear around what is and is not acceptable.

If there is a problem, then have the tough conversation quickly and nip the problem in the bud.

Then get out of their way and let them get on with it.

As they grow and progress with your business, apart from leading them in the short term, you will also need to review their progress with regular appraisals.

This allows you to provide constructive feedback about how they are going, both on the positive side and also the areas they can improve. Equally important is to give them long-term direction that they desire, that is also a win for the business, win-win.

You can also be helping them stay engaged and feel as though they are making a meaningful contribution that is fulfilling.

This is such an important part of the long-term retention of team members.

Having worked so hard to find a great team member, let's make sure we are able to keep them on board for many years to come.

# 6. CONCLUSIONS

Hopefully you have been able to get a ton of value from my book and have begun installing your own PRM, so you never have to get stressed about having to find someone if you lose a key team member.

Being in business is one of the toughest life challenges there is and I tip my hat to my fellow business owners. Whilst it can be one of the toughest things we do in life it can also be one of the most rewarding.

Having a team of dream employees working together harmoniously and with great fulfillment delivering your product and or services, has to be one of the most amazing things to experience in life.

# 7. GETTING HELP TO MAKE THIS YOUR REALITY?

I trust that you have found my book, Find Your Ideal Employee, valuable and that you are now moving towards my model of what the purpose of a business is that I described in chapter 1.

If you would like to find out more about how I help business owners like you build your dream business, you can find out more by visiting www.businessmentored.com

**To Apply To Be Mentored By Brad, Scan The Qr Code Below.**

# BOOKS BY THIS AUTHOR

**Find Your Cash**

17 Strategies to uncover the cash you are leaving on the table in your business right now.

· Use small tweaks of key figures that result in sizeable quick cash gains.
· Use the benchmark tool to compare performance to similar businesses in your industry and find where your business is bleeding unnecessary cash.
· Clearly demonstrate the impact that discounting and weak sales process has on a bank balance.
· Make better use of the current resources available to grow cash.
· Boost cash flow through better management of selected important figures.

Author and mentor Brad Flynn shares with you the his tried and true framework to Find Your Cash fast in your business, based on working with 1000's of business owners since 2010.

## How To Work On Your Business (Not Just In It)

Turn Your Business Into a Profitable Machine That Works Without You

You didn't start your business to become its most overworked employee. Yet here you are—drowning in to-do lists, putting out fires, and wondering when you'll ever catch up.

How to Work on Your Business (and not just in it) is your step-by-step guide to escaping the daily grind and building a business that thrives without your constant presence.

Inside, you'll discover:
- Proven frameworks to shift from operator to owner
- Simple strategies to systemize, delegate, and scale.
- How to reclaim your time and focus on what really moves the needle
- Real-world stories from business owners who made the leap

This book isn't theory—it's a practical playbook for business owners ready to grow, profit, and finally breathe.

Whether you're turning over $100K or $5M+, the roadmap is here. It's time to stop running on fumes—and start running a business that fuels your life.

Made in the USA
Monee, IL
28 April 2026

49136496R00036